Ou
Garden
Bench

102 Poems to Nourish the Soul

Rosalie Helene Barton

Miss Mouse Publishing House

What people are saying

In *Our Garden Bench*, which is a collection of daily written free verse poetry, Rosalie draws on her life experiences to give her readers something with which they can identify. The poems are warm and cryptic conversations with God. I found the poems well worth reading, and marvelled daily at the gifting God has given her.
Neil K, Canada

Many times Rosalie's drawings and poems have just 'hit the spot' for me. I could swear she knew exactly how I was feeling that very day.
Moira C, Scotland

Rosalie's poems tell of her pursuit of genuine freedom, and her experiencing the Father's acceptance and delight as she walks with Him. Her openness and authenticity are an invitation for all to know his love and the deep rest found only in him.
Tracy W, USA

Our Garden Bench

Rosalie's poems give me hope for each day, while reminding that I always have support and a Comforter by my side. Her language is simple and direct.
Jacqueline F, Scotland

Rosalie has such a unique and beautiful way of weaving art and words together, then entwining them into our relationship with God. Her poetry and art work always touch my heart on multiple levels.
Rachel H, Scotland

I read Rosalie's poetry because it is like listening to conversations with Jesus. I find them encouraging and often reminders of truths I need to hear.
Eric J, Canada

Dedication

To my Dad, whose limericks and other poems have always inspired me, and whose constant encouragement keeps me going.

Ebook ISBN-13:978-2-4248-3951-0
Paperback ISBN-13:978-2-9009-6024-0
Audiobook ISBN-13: 978-2-1757-0189-0

Cover design by: Rosalie Helene Barton
Editor and Formatting: Christopher Barton
Printed in the United States of America

Introduction

I have often found that writing things down helps me process what God is trying to teach me. In the last few years some of these writings have started to morph into poems, some of which I began to share with others. After receiving more and more encouraging feedback from friends I began to post them online to a wider audience.

I use my own quirky language and analogies and pictures that mean something to me. These are an authentic reflection of what I'm going through. I hope you will be inspired and comforted and find new expressions for your own spiritual journey.

Contents

Our garden bench

Our garden bench!
What's happened to our garden bench?
So clean and lovely,
Our own sanctuary of peace?

Why is there a great thorn bush
There on the side?
You can't even relax
Your head here
Without the thorns
Scratching and hurting
Your dear head.

I do not rebuke you
For letting this ugly plant
Spring up,
But it is not for our garden.

Here.
Let Me take care of it.
At my touch, it turns to dust
For it was never real anyway.
It was in your head, robbing you,
Choking out your joy.
But I bring life and peace.

Rest your head now.
Love plants grow here.
Blossoms of hope,
Stems of praise,

Trees of faithfulness.
All around,
The fragrance of goodness.

You are safe here.
Let's give our bench
A fresh lick of paint.

Limitless

I see the clouds parting,
I see the sun breaking through.
I see the birds soaring,
I see the endless horizon.
This is the sky,
This is the vastness.
This is the limitless vision.
But not even approaching
Your limitlessness,
Your abundant realm.
Your infinity,
Your beyond,
Your possibility
In my heart,
In my life.
Inside out
Tardis-like glory within.
Inner cathedral.
Greater, higher, stronger
Than anything,
Even the greatest things.
God in me,
Christ in me,
Spirit in me,
Limitless. Limitless.

Morning Rest

Morning rest
Even just a moment of breath
Joy embraced
My closest Friend is very near
Spirit closer than breath
Father's arms enfolding me

Take this time
Know it, feel it, breathe it
See the day stretched before me
Defined by this moment
Of love and being loved
Swirling with the beauty of God
Marked by His peace.

There is plenty and more

Walk with me
Through these fields
Down the road
Reach your arms out
Let your hands feel
The leaves flutter past
These are mine
There is plenty and more
And more

Rest

See the orchards
Fruit of every kind
Look at the cows
My cattle on a thousand hills
My sheep, my flocks
Livestock, happy livestock
Are mine.

I will not let you want.
Rise above, see the abundance
And know.
I have enough, I AM enough.

Pause and breathe

Step back
And look at me
See me
Know me.

What do I do?
How do I choose?
Busy, busy, busy girl
Slow down.

Choose carefully.
Then pause
Remind yourself.
Pause and breathe.
Stop and smile.

It's ok to sit down
Sip your tea
Before you do
The next thing you do.

Is it really true?

Is it really true
That I am perfect in you?

Woah – that's a big word!
We bat these other ones around quite freely:
Forgiven, sanctified, righteous, even perfected.
But perfect?
There's a real doneness in that.
A thing that lets us rest and smile.

And then the sneaky voice snivels in
With its pompous caveat:
But you're not perfect,
You can't rest on your laurels.
Anyone can see you're not.

But, as a matter of fact,
I am.
God has said I'm good.
Who's to counter that?
I am good, I have been made perfect
And I am resting in His finished work.

Pieces of the puzzle

New found
Pieces of the puzzle
Might seem small
And insignificant
But they might be pivotal
And bridge together
Big pieces that didn't look
Like they could come together before.

Some things
Gradually discovered
Carry great weight.
The time you took to find them
Is not wasted.

Open up doors

I trust in you
To open up doors
No man or woman
Dog or cat
Can shut.
Ways for me.
Openings
Solutions
And paths.

And I will go through
And smile
And know
It was you.

My mood is my mood

My mood is my mood
Not from someone else
An unwanted gift
Placed in my hands
And absorbed into my being
To define my day as it will

No, my mood is my mood
I choose
I choose whether or not to let fear in
Let anxiety rear its head
Let dread, anger, hopelessness
Set up camp
My attitude, my choice

I care
I care deeply
I listen
I empathise

But I choose
In your presence is fullness of joy
Let me find your joy here
Bear my burdens
Keep me safe
I choose thankfulness and praise
Because my mood is my mood

Plenty to share

Beautiful cupboards
Filled with rich and sundry resources to share.

Come round
And sit at my table
And I will share
The hospitality and delights of the Lord.

A little glimpse of his banquet to come.
There will always be
Plenty to share,
For every morning
His table is renewed.

Crazy drama

Woah Nelly!
What a day.
Crazy drama
All the way.

Panic
Chaos
Blind confusion
Stop, think
Find solution.

Hither thither
What to do?
Resolution
Sighing: phew!

Head is spinning
With the strain.
Drama damages
My brain.

Relief and thank yous
Come at last.
Glad to sleep
When crazy's past.

A journey of joy

How do I pass this on?
The knowledge, the wholeness,
The oneness?
Peace in chaos
Freedom from worry
The walk, the flight, the joy.

Be free
Know God,
I say to deaf ears.
Know for yourself
This goodness,
This delight.

Every valley shall be exalted
For me and for you.
God will lift up these places
Of sadness and woe
So that we can
Praise Him even here.

I can only do and speak a little
Of His goodness and kindness to me.
And hope and know
That this will spark
A journey of joy
For the listener.

It's only a blip

A blip
A blip
It's only a blip
In Your economy
In Your grand scheme of things
And if it's Your grand scheme
That makes You the Grand Schemer
A creative Genius with a twinkle in Your eye
Continually making stuff out of nothing
Ex nihilo
And making good stuff out of bad
Twisting, turning, rejigging
Adjusting, helping, aiding, mending
Until all's well
So, mend this blip
And then take me on Your lap
So together we can sit back
And admire Your work

Like fresh morning toast

Here you go.
A piece of joy
Like fresh morning toast.

Nothing beats the smell.
Mm. Savour it.
All's well.

Butter's melted.
Jam is sweet.
Little bites.
But there's more
Where that came from.

I am all about joy.
Joy, freedom, delight.
Not control, angst, stress.

Enjoy.
Know.
Everything will be well,
Little by little.
You know this.
Walk in it.

I will radiate You

Can your glory be shown in me
At home today?
On a day of rest,
Not much going on outside,
Can I display you?
Can I sparkle?
Can I dwell?
I can.
And I will.
I will do the work that I need to do.
But
I will also pause.
I will drink of your
Living water.
I will feast at your
Table of delights.
I will radiate you
Because I am in you,
And you are in me,
And I can't help it!

Nestle in

I think, to start with
I am going to nestle in
Bury my head in Your chest
And recharge.
Breathe deeply
Slow down
Relax.

I am in the safest place
The very safest place.
We can sit together
And hold hands
On Your great, wonderful,
Heavenly porch swing.
The epitome of rest.

I don't know very much
But I can relax
And I can trust
Lean on Your shoulder
And wait.

Take my little clay hands

All good things
Flow from your pen
Waft like wind from your lips
Come to life on the canvas
From your brushes
Leap off the workbench
Works of clay set free to be
Wow!
What's there to say but wow?
So take my little clay hands
Let me create like you
Works of art
Lovely pieces
Words of life
Pictures of beauty
Good things
Flowing from me
A little like they flow from You

Walk in the grace

Walk in the grace
That's for today.

Don't strain to think
Of what you really should do
Like you're trying to recover
What you were worried about
So you can worry again.

Do the things before you now
With joy in your heart
And if you really must do some
Things that fill you with dread,
Lay aside the dread
And ask for the grace and joy
To do them.

It will surely be given to you.
You will have all you need
To walk through each moment
And receive your affirmation
At the close of the day
From the Lover of your soul,
The Grace Giver himself,
As He whispers, "well done!"
And tucks you in.

Spread your petals slowly

Open up to the light.
Spread your petals slowly.
You are so delicate
And beautiful.
So loved.
And this day
Like all the rest
There will be enough
To nourish you,
To strengthen you,
To grow you.
Trust the light.
Enjoy the soil.
Drink the water.
Be.

A moment of wisdom

I sometimes need
A moment of wisdom
An opportune window
To step in
And do a little thing
I need to do

A well intentioned bull
Attempting to set foot gracefully
Into the china shop
Is still a bull
And still succeeds
In leaving mayhem behind.

I need the slowly, slowly approach.
I cannot set all to rights
With swift accuracy now.

It will be premature and clumsy.
But if I wait and listen and watch
I might catch these moments of wisdom
And do a little good at the right time
And be satisfied.

Run With Endurance

It's a 'run with endurance' kind of day
It's a run with endurance in a restful kind of way

Not a stop what I am doing
Throw my hands up in the air
Go and crawl into a cave
And then forget I even care

No, today's a day for going on,
Believing what is true
It's a day for leaning on the
Everlasting arms of you

So, that's the plan.
I guess today, I'll run a little more.
I'll step, I'll trust, I'll lean, I'll know
That good things are in store

By the river

Remember?
Do you remember
Where you are planted?
Right here
By the river
The only place.
Not a frantic place.
A calm, nourishing place.
A full, flourishing place.
You are safe here!
Listen to the wind.
Listen to the love-whispers
Be held,
Be strong!

Can anything separate me?

Has anything changed?
Am I separated from You?
Can anything separate me?
Anything?
No.
No, and I know it can't!

What if this or that gets really bad
Or really hard?
Have you withdrawn Your hand?
Hardly!

I know that nothing, nothing
Can change that.
We are together and You've promised
To stay.
Always.

I trust in Your love, Your protection,
Your provision.
Now, as always
I am in Your care.

I work from home

Hide me,
Oh hide me!
Cup my cheek
In Your hand
And fold me in.

When I can't process,
Take it all in,
Take me in.
Still my beating heart.

Tap Your rhythm
Gently on my shoulder
Until I relax
Into peace
In sync with You.

I look up into Your eyes
I don't need to step away
Into my day
I can stay.
This is home
And I work from home.

Good things

Good things
Can happen
Can begin to happen
Good things can begin to happen to you
Change your brain
Change your beliefs
Good things can and will
Begin to happen to YOU

Stride and glide

Whence cometh this exhaustion?
Why do I feel so tired, so heavy?

I compare my workload to another's.
And it's not so bad.
But for me, right now it's wearisome.

The mundane jobs and the unexpected
Complications jar me.
Hem me in.

Release me today, oh Lord.
So that I am light and happy
And I can stride and glide
With fresh perspective.
Not driven, but free,
Glad, renewed and refreshed.

Grace for this trampoline life

God, give me grace for this trampoline life
My poor brain is losing its come back
Its bounce

I'm tugged and I'm tossed from hither to yon
The ups and the downs have been taking their toll

A panic
A drama
A crisis to solve
Some desperate prayers
The watch and the wait

With trust, expectation, a dusting of doubt
And then the all's well
And I let out my breath

A swell of relief
Like a huge pent up wave
A sigh of exhaustion
A wash of emotion

My buoyancy status restored once again
A restful night's sleep before unknown today
God, give me grace for this trampoline life

An invitation

I woke today
With warmth and hope
An invitation
To begin with peace
Say yes to serenity

I looked up to see
The sun shining through my window
This was the new morning
I was craving

Let those rays penetrate
My heart
Banishing gloom and despair
Lifting my gaze to heaven
And faith
For good things to come

Get well card

Are you weary in well doing?
In well thinking, in well hoping?

Well, a get-well card is on its way
And when you open it, you'll find
New rest and energy and hope
With faith and possibility

Your batteries will be recharged
By heaven's electricity
So open up your get-well card
And wellness new will come to You.

Let your courage grow

Your victory is not a maybe.
It's a given.

You actually do have this.
You've got this!

Doing these trust exercises,
Building this hope muscle
Have not been in vain.

We do win,
You do win.
The blessed relief,
The grateful celebration
Are real.
And you can join the party early!

You can even count your chickens before they hatch. Because they all survive.

Let your courage grow
As you see the little daily signs
That God is taking care of you
His love-victory is completely secure!

Keep your chin up

Step out.
Yes, once again.
Time for your water walking workout
Out you come.
Look at you!
Those muscles are doing well.
Keep your chin up.
Keep your focal point.
I would suggest My eyes.
Yes, the storm's been turned up a bit.
A few more steps
And we'll get back into the boat.
Well done!
You've made it!
We're so proud of you!

Thank you

What is this blessing I walk in?
This delight that's mine,
This special intensity of delight,
My inheritance?

I am so favoured,
So blessed.
Could I unwrap it a little more?
Is it really meant for me, for us?

Well, thank you.
Thank you.
Let me hold you
And say thank you.

I confess
I really don't get it.
I can't wrap my head
Around its value.

Like a little child
That loves the giver
And likes the present
And doesn't understand
Money and accounts and bank cards.

But I can say thanks
And I do my very best to do that.
Thank you.
Thank you.
I am so blessed.

This is only an illusion

Where am I really standing?
It seems like I am
All alone in a gloomy corridor
A hotel hallway
Dim and dreary and endless
Monotonous in its drudgery
But I've the sense to know
This is only an illusion
A nasty delusion.

So where am I really?
Is it with you
On my sunny mountaintop?
Am I standing tall
Bathed in your rays of glory
Each one ablaze
With love, joy and possibility?

Am I surrounded by a
Billion worshippers
Angels, sons and daughters
In perpetual praise?
Is this where I am really standing?
Please say it is!

It's for real

It's time for the King to make
His very grand entrance
In my heart.

This is really
The best thing that's ever happened.
Like going to see
The biggest celebrity ever
Coming into town.

Only He takes particular notice of you.
He doesn't just sign your copy
Of His book
The poster for your bedroom wall.

But He looks over
The whole crowd of thousands
And sees you
Locks eyes with you.
Your heart leaps.
It's for real.

He steps out of his car
And runs straight over to you
Brings you back with Him
Not for a day experience
At His grand mansion
But forever.

And all your family and friends
Are invited as well.
Over the top generosity.
No disappointing at all.

You're never going to want
For anything
Ever again.

And did I mention
He meets all your emotional needs as well?

This kind treatment is for everyone.
This love is for all,
Rich and poor
Big and small.
What a celebrity
Worth celebrating.
What a King!

I trust in You

The Lord God is a sun and shield!

Time to trust in your rays
To show the wonderful truth
To me.
What's real,
What's not.

Time to trust in your protection
From all that smothers
And tries to deceive.

Time to know
That I can see clearly now
And I am kept safe.

Great Sun and Shield
I trust in You.

I'm making everything new

I'm making everything new
I love it when you say that

I let go
What a relief
Of all of yesterday's
Pain, sorrow, and disappointment
To see what you have in store
For today

I take hold of your hands
And gaze up into your
Lovely eyes
And trust you
For your new
To come to me

All is still

Daybreak in my garden
Freshness in the air

There is no striving
There is no busyness
No urgency

All is calm
I see the dew on the flowers
Crystal drops on blades of grass

Reflecting holy light

All is still
I sit on my little garden seat
I sit and wait and enjoy

Then I hear your soft footsteps coming
Smell the rich coffee you bring me
Let's sit together and drink

Today I will be with you, you say
The former things have passed away
Behold, I make all things new

I have a need to fly

Some are content to walk below
But I have a need to fly
Step out, let go, lift off, and soar
And see things from up high

Sadness, gloom, and worry drain
While hope and faith arise
Good things are possible again
When viewed from Heaven's skies

So take my hand and we will glide
We'll launch and loop above
With Holy Trinity, my guide
I'll be aloft with Love

A Clean Heart

Create in me
Something brand new
Fresh, never seen before.

Try something innovative
I'm game, always up for a change
And you're good
Good at what you do

Not one to shy away from an idea
To incorporate into your work
Inside me

And if I'm in need
Of a bit of a clear out
Go ahead.

I'll let go of the rubbish
And trust Your judgement
No time to be sentimental
With my junk.

So a clean heart
Your design
And a spirit renewal if you could, please.

I will express Your goodness
As best I can and exhibit Your work!

Thanks in advance

Hey God!
Provision opportunity here!
See me waving?
Yes, right here!
Yesterday would have worked
Just fine as well
But today is good
Too.

I won't go on about it.
You have all the figures.
Go ahead and surprise me
Like you do!

Thanks in advance.
You're good at this.
I can already feel
That happy, contented relief!

Thank you.

This is what I choose

Lift my downcast eyes
To the truth
Not lies

Up the mountain path
I'll begin
To laugh

An adventure, this
Is a life
Of bliss

Let my sadness go
And your joy
I'll know

This is what I choose
To rely
On You

I am who I am

Am I valuable?
Am I useful?
Are they the same thing?
I don't think they really are.

A spatula is really useful
But not so valuable and
Not so beautiful.

But I am who I am.
I'm beautiful for being me.

Valuable, so valuable to my Artist
More like a vase or an elegant jug.

Sometimes just sitting on the shelf
Looking pretty
Sometimes at the table
Pouring goodness into glasses.
Sometimes showing off
Arrangements of fresh flowers.

I am me
Exactly me.
And that's as it should be.

Look and Behold

Look and behold
Search and see
These are tasks
You have for me

Is that really all I have to do?
Look inside, and look at you?

Show me those eyes
Kindly met
I haven't understood them yet

But they comprehend
My hidden parts
My sadness, joy
My thoughts, my heart

So take my hands
I'll lift my face
I'll stay and stare
Linger and gaze

And if that's all I need to do
It is enough
Just knowing you

I don't look at you like that

I don't look at you like that.
Like what?
I don't look at you in the morning
Tentatively, from afar
And wait to see if you are going to
Do the things you should do,
Before I breathe out in relief
That you're still on track
And worthy of My love and approval.

No, I wait beside your bed
For you to wake up
So you can see me smiling at you.
Because I approve of you already
And you can relax.
It's okay.
My very, very precious child.
You are a diamond.

Resilient

I'm delicate, yet robust,
Vulnerable, yet resilient.
When the winds blow at me
I am not torn apart.

I will be joyful in the morning.
I will greet the sun with a laugh.
I'm made of sterner stuff
Than the storm can fling at me.

I can withstand the gale.

But yesterday's tumult is not for today.
The warmth and the light high in sky
Spell hope, life and peace for today
And I receive them readily.

Come up here

Here I am with my stuff
On my little chair
In my little room
In my little house
On my little street
In my little town
In my little country
And He sees me
Here.

But it's not where I really live.
He says the whole sky is yours
The glory of the clouds
The shining sun
The stars
The universe
The galaxy
Yours.

Live from this vast glorious place
Of My love and glory
And know that
Your stuff, your stress, your suffering
Is temporary and slight
Compared to
The higher happiness of My heaven.
Come up here.
Your home.

I'll be okay, today

Another morning to open up to.
Here I am
New energy awaits me
For today.
I may feel depleted from yesterday's battles
But I'll have enough for this day.
And if I'm lucky
I'll be able to take a few moments here and
there
To replenish
Now and then
I'll sneak in a splash of prayer
To God who's right there
I'll be okay, today.
You are beside me, within me
Around me
Above me, below me.
And I am in you!
Thank you for this very great
Provision.
All I need

Better yet, fly!

Walk and keep on walking
Glide with purpose.
Better yet, fly!

Not everyone can see your wings,
But you know that I let you rise above.
You know you can see over the mess,
The troubles, the quandaries.
So keep on.

I am your wisdom.
I am your strength
For big and small problems,
Situations where
My help is required.
Pearls of perception
Will be provided
From heaven
In a timely fashion!

On you go!
Release your heavy backpack.
I'm good at dealing with burdens.
I'll take the very best care of everything.
Here's my hand.
Let's persevere together.
I promise you,
I'll make it worth your while.

Today

I reach up my hands to You,
My heart to You.
I surrender.
I give up.
I don't know.
I don't get it.
Don't understand.
So just help me
To be faithful today
To your calling.
I can't control.
I can't make myself look good,
But I can listen
And obey, and walk with You
Today.
So that is what I'll do.

Joy maker

I take this joy
As my own
It's there to be had.

Oh glorious joy
Why do I struggle
To figure it all out
When it's all here?

Joy maker,
I enjoy indulging
In the fruits of Your craft.
Take a little wine
From the glad glass of God.

This is the day that the Lord has made
I will rejoice and be glad in it.

Take my hand

Wind, whisper my name.
Sing my song.
Let Your howling, haunting melody
Pierce straight into my soul.
I'm here
And ready to hear.

Hello, Wind.
Let me join in.
Lift my face and let my
Harmony rise with your notes,
Now a happy, dancing descant,
And then a strong, sustained alto.

Oh Wind!
I long to rise with the song!

Take my hand
And lift me
On Your currents!
Let me join the dance.

Yes!
Now I see it.
There are more of us.

Yes, thousands.
Singing with the Wind,
Flying, sweeping, weaving, spinning
Joining the dance,
singing the song
With the breeze and the clouds.

Shine on me, Sun,
And with all that's in me
I will bless and dance and sing!

I can relax

This is where the truth is spoken.
Let Truth be a comforting word here
Like Blanket or Cosy.
Because the truth is good.

Just as I am
God loves me.
God loves us
And is taking care of us
Not because we have
Done it all right
Remembered everything
Or been super faithful
But just because He loves us
Spots and all.

The truth is
I can relax.
Oh soul, trust in God!
You don't have to make it happen.
Just step into
This great faithfulness
Thankfulness
Already reality realm
Where joy, bliss and gratitude abound!

Ginger for some zing!

These cookies need some spice.
After blandness,
A little flavour, please.

Show me these little nuances
Of blessing.
They are already there, but oh
I need my eyes opened again,
My taste buds titillated
To all the wonderful flavours
Of my life.

Kind, constant vanilla.
Reliably basic with its sweetness.
Cinnamon, comforting and fragrant.
Ginger for some zing!
Lemon lends its zest.

I'm so blessed.
There is so much more.
Pops of colour
Enticements of fragrance
Sizzles of flavour.
My life isn't a bland biscuit.
I have a lot of reason to sing
While I zing!
Thank you!

Night time mind

Finally, peace settles over me.
Why do you wander,
Night time mind
Over empty plains
And fruitless fretful
Barren terrain?

The place to be is the knee
The lap of God.
The place for my head
Is against your chest
Where the beat of your heart
Is calm and tranquility to me.

Each breath of mine is a gift
You weave and blow
Through me.
I am still and quiet now
Like a satisfied child.
No agitation,
No anxiety,
Only rest.

You're mine

This is not how it works.
You sitting in the waiting room
Wondering if I'll see you
If your application will be
Successful
If it met with My approval.
Second guessing yourself
Should I have said this?
Should I have said that?
"No," I laugh, as I pick you up
Off the floor, where you were playing waiting room.

"Come, sit on my lap, look at my eyes!
I approve of you.
Look at this room, this big house.
Look out the window at my estate.
You're mine, and this is
All yours too.
All is well, and you are
Well provided for."

Fixing your eyes

Well done, little one!
Well done!
You did well trusting Me
Through the night.
Now, this is the morning.
The morning, when light
Breaks through darkness,
When shadows melt
And beams of glory
Dissolve doubt.
I have seen you looking at Me
In the dark
When you couldn't see Me
But you refused to turn away
Fixing your eyes
As I taught you
For the joy set before you.
Believe me, I was delighted
And I couldn't wait till the Morning
To lift your hand
Lift your chin
Let you see hope again.
Well done, I say.
Your perseverance is not in vain
All my promises will be fulfilled
In you,
For this is the morning.

Too much

I know you said
It would never be too much
But yesterday felt like it was
Too much.

I felt battered. I felt bruised.

Time to rise on
The wings of my Dove.

Lift me up, dear Dove.
Let me rise, let me soar.
Away on your glorious winds.

I nestle in for the ride.
High above the calamity
My place of safety.

My little creator

Did someone say
To stop dreaming?
In the name of contentment
And living in the present?

Well, don't stop.
Oh, please don't stop!
It's your dreams
That are so delightful.

Colours on a canvas
So fanciful and free
Brushstrokes no one else
Can see
Or make.
A thankful canvas,
A blueprint,
A scaled down model
For a wonderful life!
I love to create and breathe
With you, my dearest dreamer.

Be my painter,
Be my sculptor,
My little creator.
More, not less, with gratefulness.
Anticipation, contentment
And joy!

Glorious breath

This weariness, this slog
The tiresome trudge of today
Could You lift it a little, please?

Mental flutter, be stilled
Busy hands, relax
Hither-thither feet, stretch out.
Time to inhale, exhale
Fill my lungs with glorious
Breath.

Let Your tender hands brush away tears
Smooth away tension
Let the sweetest, kindest voice
Whisper 'well done'
Into my ears.
Whether or not
I think I deserve it.

Wash away the sting of pain.
Sing Your song of hope
Straight into my heart
Awakening belief again.
I nestle in for this rest.
For this day,
And for every day.

Behold, I make all things new!

Behold, I make all things new!
Look! That's what He does!
Old, worn out, stressful stuff
Becomes fresh, new, peaceful stuff!
Anticipation replaces dread!
Cheeky smiles creep up
With the realisation
That this goodness
Will completely overwhelm
The darkness.

Light, love and zest
Will overcome
The grey, pervasive fog.
Run, flee from His presence,
Doubts and fears!
Rise up and welcome to you, Hope!
November gloom give way
To May morning expectancy!
I let go
And I take hold of
This newness
Freely given.
Gratefully received.

Flick the Switch

When did I get so used to dread?
When did I start expecting the worst?
What made me start bracing myself
For sorrow and disappointment?

This has to stop.
I need you to flick the switch.

Hope never disappoints.
Love never fails.
Goodness and mercy
Are running after me.
Wherever I go, wonderful things happen!
These things are true.

I let You
Reset me.
Here I am.
Change my mind.
I repent.
Think it over again.
The steadfast love of the Lord
Never ceases.
My default is this.
I can't wait to see what
You will do!

Each step for You

Each step is holy
Even the stumbles.
I'm trying I'm learning
And I'm leaning.

Oh, the delight on Your face!
It's sacrilegious to strain and try to make
You happy by some sort of
Effort on my part.

At this point, I know!
For goodness' sake, I know!
I know you love me
Without condition.

I know you approve of me!
I know you don't narrow
Your eyes in disapproval
Or wag your angry finger.

I am Your beloved.
I am Your child.
You always have a hug for me.
An encouraging glance.

You always help me.
You always lift me up.

So today, I trust in You.
Help me to trust in You.
Let me feel Your delight
And teach me to walk
Each step for You.

Soar!

It's a time for looking up,
A time for rising up,
A time for taking off and flying.

Take me across the skies
On Your wings of wind.

No excuse or hesitation.
I need this!
I need to get out more.
And by getting out I mean UP!

Up above
Where nothing is impossible
And all comes out right.

Soar!
Be lifted up.
This is the time for it.
For great courage, great faith
A leap of love and bravery.
Complete trust in You.

I will not fall, but even if I do,
You will catch me!

Good job

Well, I think you did well.
Telling myself here:
Good job.
You held on.
You kept your eyes more or less
Above the waves.
And when they dipped down
For a second, for a brief moment
You didn't beat yourself up about it.
No.
You let Love lift you up again.

Because it's almost more important
How you recover,
Than never falling
In the first place.
You didn't let the night crash in on you
With all its horror stories.
You kept singing and gazing and believing.
And now, in the morning, keep trusting
Because last night was real
And you did well.

This is me

I am kissed by sunlight.
Rays of love warm me.
I am me.

Truly happy.
I curl my lips into a smile

This is me
In You
On my journey.

Inhale, exhale

Why a cup of tea?
What is the point?
It takes a moment.
More than a moment.
You can't just guzzle it down.
You have to take your time.

Even making it.
No rushing the brew.
Let the leaves steep through.

Then sip and savour
Little by little.
So different than the rush
The normal rush of life.
But then, what's normal?

I want to live in the sips
The breaths
The knowing.
I look to You with longing
And contentment.
I slow and still my soul.

Inhale, exhale.
Inhale, exhale.
Let myself
Dawdle, not dash.

Open my eyes

Every step, blessed.
Every movement, holy.
Every word, every thought,
Worship, praise, thanksgiving.
You are in all, through all.
Every breath, divine.
Lovely Holy Spirit,
Open my eyes,
My ears,
My senses
To You this day
So that I will know this deeply
And do my day
This way
For love and glory.

Rosli 23

Easy and light

Give it away
The heaviness, the burden
The cumbersome backpack
You think you need to carry
Just to be responsible
In a barely minimal way.

This just isn't true.
We have an invitation
For rest
From a gracious Inviter.

He's not too busy to lift
It off our shoulders
And give us His light load.

Easy and light.
Easy and light.
His words, not mine.

I for one
Am letting go
And taking up this invitation

Lift me skyward

This is a flying day.
Prepare for lift off.
Will I do it?
Yes.
It's where I am
Just because you invited me

Some days, I walk on water.
Some days, I glide with joy.
Some days, hesitantly tippy-toe.
Some days, I barely move.

It's okay. I'm always, always in You.
I live and move and breathe in You!
But today, I fly.

Lift me skyward.
Lift me heavenward.
My worship is my flight.
I rise above
And ride the wind
With You.

I take this adventure.
Say yes.

So much provision

So much provision
So much help
Should I be surprised?
Guess not.

Of course He is here
Of course He's my dad
I have nothing to worry about.

Thank you for all Your
Good and perfect gifts.

Let my heart rest once again.
No striving
Just gratefulness and assurance.

All things work together
And I have all I need.
There it is.
Amen.

You were made to fly

Untie those silly strings tethering you to the ground. You were made to fly.
Let your feet come away.
Lift off.
Above it.
Feel your spirit come to life.
Feel the stress drain away.
Look at the clouds.
They are in no hurry.
Simply being
Cottony and pleasant
In the blue sky.
Yes, the sky is blue.
Forget not My benefits.
Who has provided for you?
Who has been your Companion?
Who has sung to you?
Who has lifted you above?
Your Creator knows your name.
Your Creator calls you to this
Vast, open blue.
Sorrow may last for the night,
But joy, great joy,
All-encompassing joy comes
In the morning.
And you will not miss out.

Rosalie

I welcome your wind

Just a little breath,
A little breeze in the morning
Lifts my spirits,
Blows away blues
Wafts away worries.

Nighttime threats and thoughts,
Convoluted musings, struggling
To become hopes and prayers
Under cover of darkness
Untangle themselves
Quite naturally in the daylight,
Transforming into possibility.

Looming clouds shift into
Innocuous cotton.

Breathe on me, breath of God,
Breather of all things good.
I welcome your wind
Over my day.

Yes. Always enough.

There really is enough.
Plenty
For everything
For needs fulfilled
For hearts' desires
For blessing others.
Yes. Always enough.

Whether it's a treasure hunt
To search out
Or handed to us on a platter.
He's still our Father.
Every good and perfect gift
Comes from Him
And we trust for these
From His generous heart
Today.

You are my hope

Fill my heart with expectation
My tummy with anticipation
You are my hope
The one whose strong arms
Reach down and
Lift me away up
Daily

Up above the stuff of darkness Below
Skyward to the stuff of heaven
My eyes really are fixed on You

I look straight into Your eyes
Straight into Your heart
Kindness, goodness, joy and life
Are there in You,
Are here in me.

Because as I stare at You.
I can't help but become,
Adjust, transform
Into this glorious one
I am meant to be.
No more distraction
Be my fixation
My obsession
Jesus.

Security is tight

I'm setting up
A rather rigorous routine
For thoughts who wish
To enter my head.

Security is tight
And they must pass
Through
My checkpoint
Past the bouncer.

He's got his standards
And every thought must meet them
Or He bounces them right out the door again.

I'm having a party inside this brain of mine
With Happiness, Hope and Life
And I don't entertain thoughts
That look more like fear and gloom.

They come, they go,
No guilt, no shame.
But those that get to stay
Are good thoughts
Heavenly thoughts
Surely, goodness and mercy.

A little choice

A choice
A little choice
To step into wonder
Funny, how choosing to see
Makes me see more clearly
What's already there

The spiritual
The heavenly
The glory realm is real
The unseen more than the seen

The mundaneness, drudgery
Gives way to bright adventure
When I look at Light Himself

Slowly, slowly

Get it all done,
Do it right away
Don't forget a single thing
It's your responsibility.

Get it all done,
Do it right away
Don't forget a single thing
It's your responsibility.

This rush
This craziness
This stress
My mental alarm clock.

But no! Stop!
Look out the window.
I see the clouds wafting by
As they should,
Each in its place
No hurry right now.

The little tree outside
My window
A place for each branch,
Each tiny twig.

Dewdrops sparkling
Drinking in the morning
Sunlight, gentle breeze.

Slowly, slowly
The day comes to the garden.

Come, busy mind.
Slow your pace.
Adopt this quiet,
Measured pace
One thing at a time.

Mind of Christ
Still my thoughts.
Tranquility
Descend.

Your rays of light
Penetrate my confusion
Compulsion, obligation
Till peace reigns again.

Help me to see

This is the great hall of the King
Wide and vast
Light streaming out from the throne
Out the windows
I find I can look
Straight at the Son
For I shine too
With his rays.

I am alone
On these polished tiles
Gazing, admiring, worshiping.
Or so I thought.

On second glance
(and how could I have missed this)
There are thousands.
Loving, praising, celebrating.
They get me!
They understand my joy.

I skip out onto the streets of the city.
There are more of us there.
We understand each other.
We all cheer for the King.

We just have to glance at each other.
And we know.
We love the King.

These are my cloud of witnesses.
Help me to see
The saints here and now
And gone before
All after the same goal.
The glory of the King.

Chill

Chill.
Slow down.
Listen.
Watch.
Know.
And be thankful,
So thankful.
No time to gripe,
Moan,
Complain.
No.
God is good
Still good.
So I will
Still
Chill.

A little rumpled

Pressed, but not crushed.
Not completely crushed.
A little rumpled.
Well, very rumpled.

Unrumple me, please!
I need Your ease.
I need Your arms.
I need Your strength.

I need that!
Yes, that.
The feeling that I am
Surrounded
By Father and Son and Spirit
And all is well
And will be well.

Beauty

Beauty
You call me a beauty.
Still can't really wrap my head
Around that.
But You love Your Son.
And You made me beautiful too
Like Him.
I can't really live like a dandelion
When You see a rose.
I am tall and fragrant
And a beauty, You say.
I smile up at You
And I begin to know it.

Because of Your smile

I look up for my morning smile;
Your smile gives me courage.
Your face gives me strength.
Your voice is sweetness itself.

Gives me
Lightness of heart,
Lightness of step.
You say, "well done."
And in that moment I realise
That yesterday's
Concerns and mistakes
Are washed away.

Tomorrow's worries
Are not mine to take care of
Right now.

I can walk through this day.
I may even have moments
Of floating through this day
Because of Your smile,
Your face,
Your voice.

Eyes upward

Straight in there
Jump on lap
Head against chest
Ear against heart

Let my heartbeat match
Yours
I think mine was going
A little fast there
Slow down

You smooth my hair
Wrap a little tendril round
Your finger
Whisper peace
Before other thoughts
Can take root

Listen
Pay attention to
The Prince of Peace

Still your mind
Breathe
Your inheritance is secure

Hands held., eyes upward
All is well

Barton 11

I will get there

When the normal road signs
Are torn up by recent storms
Flapping in the wind
No help at all
And I start to stagger and scramble,
I remember the Way, Truth and Life.
I know I am in the right path
I can't go far wrong
When I travel like this
In You
With You
And all this great family cloud.

Laying down
Fear, distraction, extra weight
Running when I can
Walking, sometimes fumbling
With determination
Resilience
Perseverance.
I will get there
And there will no more hint of a
Veil between us.
I forget sometimes it's
Already gone.
So close,
My running Companion
You are all the direction I need.

Open up the gates

Open up the gates.
My eyes, to see what's already here.
The King's dwelling,
His regal palace,
Here in my heart.
Look and see.

Open up the gates.
My ears to hear
Sounds of the kingdom
In me, around me.
Kindness, goodness
Love at work
Listen and hear.

Open up the gates
My mind to believe
My soul to feel
My heart to perceive
The King of Glory
The very One
Is here.
Look, listen and know

Always

A thousand gifts a day
Come my way
Awaken the thank you
In my heart
To see these blessings
Friends, blessings, kind words,
Thoughtful gifts.
Wow.
Little signs and big signs
That I am loved.
The things I see
The things I hear
Observed, taken in
Through the filter of Your love.
Big, wide, endless
And here.
Always.
Thank You.

You seem to have a way with words

I saw a shopping bag that said
That good things happen every time you shop.
I thought perhaps it ought to say
That good things happen every
time you stop.

'Cos when I pause and
Let You speak into my heart
When I am feeling stressed,
That moment in a crazy day
You have a way of giving me
Your rest.

You seem to have a way with words,
You speak the secret language of my soul.
In unexpected ways you come
And whisper kindly, gently to console.

Yes, good things happen every time
I stop and let You burst into my day
So be so kind and please remind
Me constantly to make a break away.

Not for what I do

Do You appreciate me?
I just need to hear it today.
You love me for me
Not for what I do
Not for how perfectly
I do it or don't do it
You laugh and say,
"Good job!"
"You're great!"
And "I love you!"
Well, I love you too,
And I crave Your encouragement today.
Thank You for loving me!

He's a great Doctor

I have this really great Doctor.
Like a really great Doctor.
Off the charts holistic.
He has a big estate
With grounds we can walk through together.
Sometimes we do that when I come to meet
Him.
He has time for proper appointments.
I can tell Him anything
And get off track
And He doesn't seem to mind.
He encourages it and even laughs with me.
He doesn't judge me,
Well, He judges the situation.
He diagnoses the problem.
We talk about what to do next.
But I never feel heavy about it.
Or shamed.
I get the feeling He wants it to work.
And He makes me feel like it's possible for
things to get better.
Oh, and the costs are covered.
I'm not sure how it all works.
I don't ask.
I just make sure to say thank you;
I don't forget all His benefits.
Excuse me if I come across a bit obsessed.
I kinda am.
He's a great Doctor.

Your acceptance

It's not as if You require perfection
For satisfaction
Love, Affection
Affirmation
You don't need it
You can see it
See me, know me
Understand me
As I am with spots and all
When I'm upright, when I fall
Why I'm trying to impress you
Is beyond me
Kind of pointless
Your acceptance
Overshadows
Faults and fails and
Flops and foibles.
You forgive me
Find me flawless
Help me to let me
Off the hook
To be less self-demanding
Let me be just where
I'm standing
While lifting me to higher places
But I don't need to win the races
Show me, let me know what grace is

This is my inheritance

Wide.
It's a big land
I could never imagine.

Limitless.
It keeps going
Around the corner to the horizon.

Plentiful.
So much to see and do.
Rich in goodness and light.

This is my inheritance.

We have been rescued

All things reconciled.
Turned back to face and love
The glorious Maker.
A happy resurrection.

We have been rescued
From death to life.
Oh frabjous day
Kalloo kallay.
Jesus has breathed
Life into our deadness
And everything
Is finding its joy in Him
Once more.

Along the way

Well done
Good and faithful
Is not just my end goal
The final stamp of approval
I live for
But words of encouragement
Along the way

My Author and Perfector
Runs with me
And He'll make sure
I get there
In the end

I am new

It's not
Trying and striving
And pushing and pulling
To get there.

I am - I am already in.
I am - I am already accepted
I am new

But I do happily
Push aside these distractions
To rush into
Glorious communion
I delightedly bound ahead
To be
Wrapped up in love.

I will not fear

Do not fear.
You say it a lot
Because I do
And sometimes almost do
And sometimes I catch myself in time
And avoid it altogether.

Fear of shame
Fear of disapproval
Fear of tut tut
Without being understood.
Lies I need you
To refute once again.

You have lifted me up
In a glory beyond shame
You have approved of me
And your voice to me
Is the encouragement to keep going.

The nodding understanding
The lovely affirming
Yes and amen.
And I will not fear
Any other voices.
I will turn your volume up full.

Lift me up

I'm worn out,
Tired
A little pitiful,
A little sad.
You think something's happening
And then it doesn't.
And you're sad
Self pity
Isn't pretty
But just for a minute.
It's okay, innit?
Lift me up
And out
And over
I am over this.
I need Your kiss,
I need Your bliss.
And I am here
With you
In the present
Moment
Don't forget,
Don't forget.
Be renewed
And let
Thankfulness
Replace
Gloom.

Holy Space

Hide me in that secretest
Of very secret places
Deep within your heart
Where we can look into
One another's faces.

And I can explain
Without being a nuisance
And you don't complain
Empathising so truly.

I don't need to clarify,
You just understand
When I need a listening ear
Not a reprimand.

This invisible comfort-place,
My undercover shelter
Takes my heart, and sets it right
When I am helter-skelter.

Don't need to justify
Over explain
Back track
There's no shame

You get it, know me
Comprehend
You're the very very best
Of all the very best friends.

And I will take the time to rest
And be refreshed
Let go of stress
Give up my mess
In this, the very secret place
The holy space
Of face to face.

This is how we do it!

I could go down the pathways
Of what could happen
And how awful it could be,
But that's not how we do it.

I could walk along
And look around the corner
To see nasty surprises that haven't even happened
But that's not how we do it.

This is what we do:
We rise above
We see things that are not yet
As if they were already
We call them out.

We feel our hope expand and grow
We know,
believe and trust and feel
These joyful things that will be real.

We walk by faith and not by sight
Until they come to pass indeed!
We don't know how
It will happen, but
This is how we do it!

We know You.
We know Your goodness
That does not stop
And never fails.

We know who we are
Your kids, with You
And we trust for the very best
Of outcomes.

We could conceive
Imaginary doom and gloom
But that's not how we do it.
This is what we do:
We trust in You.

To Your Heart

In the middle of the storm
Is a safe little place
I like to go.
A heart shaped place of calm
Where the wind doesn't blow.

And the rain doesn't fall
And I'm warm and dry
And I can just lie
And breathe.
I might even cry.

But not for very long,
Just as long as I need.
I hear sweet melodies
Soothing songs
To still my troubled soul
And restore my peace.

Take me by the hand
And lead me there again
To Your heart.

Getting There

There is no contest
No competition
I need to win
To get there the quickest
Doing the most
In the most perfect way
Looking the best
The busiest
The most efficient
The most productive
The humblest
The most confident.

No contest.
I can be
I can walk
In the easy
In the challenging
With grace,
I hope,
And a little smile.
At least a little smile.

I keep going
And I don't worry
About the hurry.
I will get There in the end
Wherever There may be.

A little wisdom

A little wisdom, if it's possible
Remind me to ask
In those situations where
It's called for
And then give me the courage
To act on it

In my thoughts
In my words
In my actions

Help me
Help me access this beautiful thing called
Wisdom

Goodness
Light
peace
Life
Love
DRAW near TO God and he will draw near to you
Delight yourself in the LORD
the fragrance of the Holy Spirit
THE KING DELIGHTS IN YOUR TRESSES
Rosalie

I am me and You are You

Face to face
Holy conversation
No mask of pretence
No mask of protection
I am me and You are You
And I am included
There is no striving
Full acceptance, full freedom
I let go and relax
Fully relax
Because I can
I don't need to try to be
Some superwoman version of me
I am me and You are You
And I am included
Not as a foster child
Till my situation improves
But as a full-fledged child
Even a friend
Too much to get, to grasp
But it's true
I am me and You are You
And I am included

About the author

Rosalie Barton

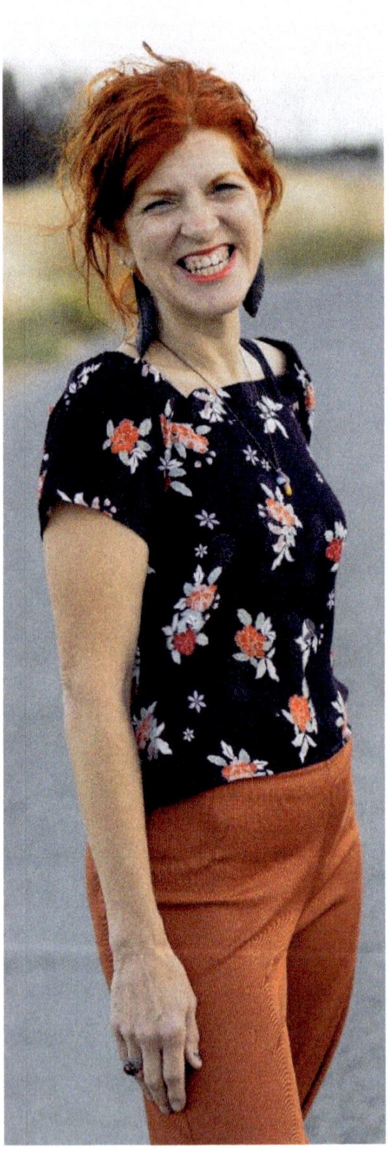

Rosalie is a Canadian and Scottish dual citizen, currently living in sunny Cyprus. Married to Chris, they have three wonderful children and one fabulous son-in-law.

She loves creating through drawing, painting, music, food, and poetry. Always looking for the beauty and love in everyday life, Rosalie sees these things as gifts from God.

Rosalie offers a glimpse into her life and spiritual journey through her daily poems and artwork.

Coffee with Rosalie

You might find Rosalie walking or running along the seafront in Larnaca, Cyprus, or enjoying an oat milk latte with friends in one of the many coffee shops; art supplies filling the table as she works on her latest piece of art or poetry! If you want to join her, by all means get in touch by email or DM and arrange a coffee!

If you aren't visiting Cyprus any time soon, but are interested in seeing more of Rosalie's poetry and artwork then you can find her online as well:

Website: www.rosalieworld.com

Instagram.com/rosaliebarton

Facebook.com/aspotofpositivity

Books coming soon

Look out for these lovely themed poetry collections, with meditations, artwork and thought provoking questions. We're curating some of Rosalie's poems into different topics for a month long of daily readings.

Becoming - If you are needing a bit more self-acceptance in your life (who doesn't?!) then enjoy these 30 days of poems, artwork, questions, thoughts, space to journal, prayers and meditations to help your heart and spirit be lifted up.

Breathe - Don't let your heart be brought low by the worries and stresses of the day. Breathe in the breath of God as you take time to rest, led by Rosalie's poems, artwork and thoughts. Ideal for night time to settle your heart, or to prepare yourself for the day ahead!

Learning to fly - Change your perspective to a heavenly one! Don't be dragged down, caught in the mud when you can be flying with Holy Spirit. Let your spirit take flight with these hope-filled, life-giving poems.

Excerpt from Becoming

I think I grew up thinking that I put my foot in my mouth a lot! I even think I remember learning the expression and thinking it was a family trait! I don't think I do it quite as often now, but now and again I do. I can either say something silly or do something I wish I hadn't. But really, I can't get paralysed by that! I have to forgive myself and go on. It happens. And someday I'll either forget the whole thing or just have a laugh!

Love,
Rosalie

Digging a hole

I do my best
To be the best
To balance myself
To choose the right thing
Talk the right way
Treat people well
But then I do a thing
That makes me cringe
In retrospect
And I feel

Like I'm sitting in
A mud puddle
And I can't explain
The dirt on my clothes
Without digging a hole
With a whole lot more mud.
Just need to say,
Oh well,
Get up and laugh
And do my best again.
Laugh, I say
Forgive yourself.
You're not perfect
And neither are they
Let's keep walking,
Learn from our stumbles
Be slow to regret,
Quick to get over it
And enjoy the journey.

Excerpt from Breathe

Breathe. You are resting in His shelter, in His shadow. I like to think of His arm around me and my head on His shoulder. That's a good place to live from. Always. We don't have to be more driven than God. He will give us our rhythm. Less driven, more rhythm!

Love,
Rosalie

Dwelling here

Dwelling here
In the shelter of the Almighty
Is where I'll be
For the foreseeable future

I have chosen this place
And I may as well stay.

The best use of my energy
Is rest
And trust

I abide, I rest, I remain
And You aren't changing

Or becoming less faithful.

No.

I can rely on that for sure.
So here I am
And here I'll be
It works for me
And I'm just taking You up
On Your kind invitation.

Excerpt from Learning to fly

Do you know me by now? I love flying and to me, it's more than metaphorical. I have had so many dreams about it. I imagine being with Jesus, high above it all. It helps. I get perspective. He lifts me up and I know I'm going to be okay. Think of it as a parent lifting the child up and swinging them around. The feeling of joy and freedom. I don't have any problem with letting my heavenly Father do that with me!

Love,
Rosalie

A Flying Holiday

Take me on a flying holiday
Where I can see your world
As I soar, swoop, sail
Over it all.
Freedom, flood through me.
I am not bound
To the ground.
Circumstances don't hold
Me captive.
Don't overpower my spirit.
I am free,
Released to rise.
In this moment
I am lifted.

Printed in Dunstable, United Kingdom

70303464R00097